Story Elemen

Using Literature to Teach Literary Elements

For Grades 3–6

Setting

Style

Characterization

Tone

Theme

Mood

Plot

...and more!

Written by Rebecca Stark

Illustrated by Karen Birchak

Educational Books 'n' Bingo

ISBN 978-1-56644-532-0

© 2016 Barbara M. Peller, also known as Rebecca Stark

Printed in the United States of America.

TABLE OF CONTENTS

TO THE TEACHER

It is important that students learn to analyze and interpret the literature they read—not only for good results on standardized tests, but also for enjoyment throughout their lives. To get the most out of what they read, they should be able to analyze a work's literary elements. This book is designed to help students in grades three through six achieve that goal.

This book includes the following:

- Plot and Conflict

- Character

- Setting

- Point of View

- Tone

- Mood

- Style

- Theme

- Genre

I hope your students and you enjoy the journey into the world of fine literature.

OBJECTIVES

Students will ...

- infer the setting of a story;

- understand the devices and word choices that help develop the mood and tone of a story;

- understand the elements of plot, including conflict, foreshadowing, flashback and resolution in a story;

- understand the characters in a story;

- infer the characteristics and qualities of the main characters in a story;

- identify the point of view and narrative voice of the story;

- determine the mood of a story;

- determine the tone of a story;

- determine the style of a story;

- identify the theme of a story;

- identify the genre of a story; and

- understand and develop story elements in their own writing.

FORMAT

Each Literary Element Section includes ...

- Definition / Explanation

- One or More Examples in Classic or Modern Literature

- Skill-building Activities Based on the Story Element

COMMON CORE STANDARDS

Key Ideas and Details

CCSS.ELA-LITERACY.RL.3.1, 4.1, 5.1, 6.1

Quote accurately from a text when explaining what the text says explicitly and when drawing inferences from the text.

CCSS.ELA-LITERACY.RL.3.2, 4.2, 5.2, 6.2

Determine a theme of a story, drama, or poem from details in the text; summarize the text.

CCSS.ELA-LITERACY.RL.3.3, 4.3, 5.3, 6.3

Compare and contrast two or more characters, settings, or events in a story or drama, drawing on specific details in the text.

Craft and Structure

CCSS.ELA-LITERACY.RL.3.6, 4.6, 5.6

Describe how a narrator's or speaker's point of view influences how events are described.

Integration of Knowledge and Ideas

CCSS.ELA-LITERACY.RL.3.9, 4.9, 5.9, 6.9

Compare and contrast the themes, settings, and plots of stories written by the same author about the same or similar characters (e.g., in books from a series).

Range of Reading and Level of Text Complexity

CCSS.ELA-LITERACY

By the end of the year, read and comprehend literature, including stories, dramas, and poetry at the high end of the text complexity band independently and proficiently.

Story Elements

About Plot

Plot is the sequence, or order, of causal events. As the name implies, a **causal event** is one that *causes* something to happen. In other words, it leads to another event. Recognizing causal events helps the reader understand *why* things occur in the story.

PLOT DEVELOPMENT

Plot describes the structure of a story. The way an author structures a story may vary, but this chart shows the main parts of plot development.

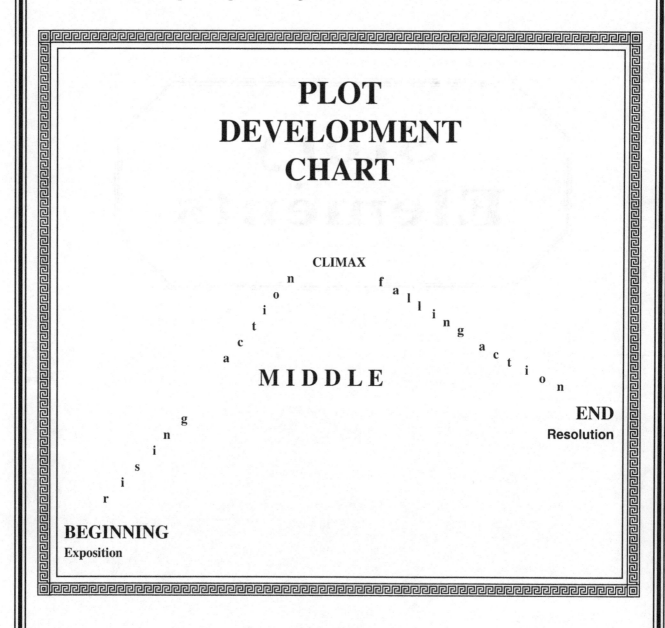

BEGINNING: *Exposition*

The beginning of the story is called the **exposition.** It is here that the author usually provides important information about the setting and the main characters. This information helps readers understand the story.

MIDDLE: *Rising Action, Climax, and Falling Action*

The protagonists, or main characters, encounter several conflicts and crises in this section, including a central conflict, or problem. Without conflict of some sort there would be no plot. **Rising action** comprises all of the events that result from the conflict. These events describe the roadblocks to the solving of the problem. The moment at which the story reaches the greatest conflict is called the **climax. Falling action** comprises the events following the climax.

END: *Resolution*

Finally, the conflict is resolved. The resolution may or may not be positive. Another word for this part of the story is *denouement*.

NOTE: Some sources put falling action in this section.

PLOT DEVELOPMENT: Narrative Order
CHRONOLOGICAL ORDER

The sequence of events in a story is also called its **narrative order.** Most of the literature you read will probably be in **chronological order.** In other words, events will be described in the same order as the order in which they occur.

FLASHBACK AND FORESHADOWING

Although most stories are told in chronological order, authors sometimes interrupt that order by using techniques such as flashback and foreshadowing. **Flashback** provides a means of telling readers about something that happened in the past. This past event should have something to do with events that have happened or will happen in the main sequence of events. **Foreshadowing** hints at things yet to occur in the story.

Plot Development in the Story of Cinderella

The following is based upon Charles Perrault's version of this classic fairy tale.

BEGINNING

Readers are introduced to main characters and the setting.

EXPOSITION

Cinderella lives with her father, her stepmother, and her two stepsisters. Her stepmother and stepsisters force her to live like a servant in her own home.

****

RISING ACTION

The prince's messenger announces that all the ladies of the household are invited to the prince's ball.

Cinderella wishes that she, too, could attend the ball.

MIDDLE

The characters' day-to-day routines change because of the prince's invitation.

Cinderella's fairy godmother uses her magic to provide all Cinderella needs in order to go to the ball, but she warns her to leave before midnight.

The prince falls in love with Cinderella and asks her to return to the ball the next evening.

The next evening she returns; however, she leaves late and loses one of her glass slippers while running away.

The prince declares he will marry the girl whose foot fits the glass slipper and sends a messenger to try it on every girl he finds.

CLIMAX

The messenger comes to the house where Cinderella lives. Although her step-family tries to thwart her efforts, Cinderella manages to get to the messenger before he leaves.

FALLING ACTION

Cinderella tries on the shoe and it fits. The messenger takes her to the palace.

Cinderella and the prince marry.

****

THE END

RESOLUTION, OR DENOUEMENT

Cinderella becomes a princess. She and the prince live in the palace happily ever after.

Cinderella, who is very kindhearted, allows her cruel stepsisters to stay in the palace too.

Causal Events

It is important to remember that plot is not merely a sequence of random events. It is a sequence, or chain, of **causal events**. In other words, every event in the plot is both the result of a previous event and the cause of a future event.

EXAMPLES FROM LITERATURE:

My Summer of the Swans, by Betsy Byars
The following events occur in this story:

> Sara's brother Charlie has a mental illness.

> A button is missing from Charlie's pajamas.

> Charlie wants to see the swans.

> Charlie gets lost.

The above statements are merely a list of events. Notice the difference, however, when they are seen as part of cause-and-effect relationships:

> Sara's brother Charlie has a mental illness; this illness causes him to become very upset when he sees that a button is missing from his pajamas. Because he is upset, he can not sleep and keeps thinking about the swans Sara showed him earlier. He decides to go on his own to see the swans, but because he is easily confused, he gets lost.

The Tale of Despereaux, by Kate DiCamillo
Notice the cause-and-effect nature of this sequence of events. In other words, notice how one event leads to another.

> The sound of the **king's music led** Despereaux to get **closer** to it and finally **reveal himself** to the king and the princess.

> Despereaux's **brother saw** the princess pat Despereaux's head and **told** their father.

> **When** Despereaux's **father learned** of his son's unmouselike behavior, he **called a meeting** of the Mouse Council.

> The **Mouse Council voted** to **put Despereaux in the dungeon.**

Cause and Effect Match-up

Complete each plot statement by choosing an effect from the following list. Write the letter that comes before the effect on the line.

EFFECTS

A. Prince Brat is disappointed in his whipping boy's behavior.

B. they will live forever.

C. the rats have become extremely intelligent.

D. Willy decides to enter the National Dogsled Race to try to win the money.

E. Lincoln draws a colon after the word "SLOW."

F. he becomes one of five children to get a tour of the candy factory.

G: the manager of the store thinks the dog belongs to Opal.

H: he does not want to return the dog to its owner.

CAUSES

_____ 1. The rats of NIMH are objects of scientific experimentation; therefore, _____.

_____ 2. Charlie finds a golden ticket in his chocolate bar; therefore, _____.

_____ 3. Jemmy did not cry when punished in place of the prince; therefore, _____.

_____ 4. Marty is sure that the dog he has found has been abused; therefore, _____.

_____ 5. The Tuck family drank water from a magic spring; therefore, _____.

_____ 6. Grandfather needs $500 to pay his taxes; therefore, _____.

_____ 7. The dog came right to her when she called him; therefore, _____.

_____ 8. The sign read "SLOW CHILDREN AT PLAY"; therefore, _____.

The following list tells on which novel each is based:

Cause #1: *Mrs. Frisby and the Rats of NIMH,* by Robert C. O'Brien

Cause #2: *Charlie and the Chocolate Factory,* by Roald Dahl

Cause #3: *The Whipping Boy,* by Sid Fleischman

Cause #4: *Shiloh,* by Phyllis Reynolds Naylor

Cause #5: *Tuck Everlasting,* by Natalie Babbitt

Cause #6: *Stone Fox,* by John Reynolds Gardiner

Cause #7: *Because of Winn Dixie,* by Kate DiCamillo

Cause #8: *The Higher Power of Lucky,* by Susan Patron

Sequence of Events:
The Whipping Boy

In Sid Fleischman's tale of switched identities, the prince and his whipping boy are mistaken for one another. Use context clues to put the events in chronological order. Number them from 1 to 16.

_____ Prince Horace explains to the king what really happened; Jemmy and Prince Horace are now friends.

_____ Jemmy is whipping boy to Prince Horace, known as Prince Brat. The two look alike.

_____ Jemmy realizes that they think he is the prince, so he pretends to be Prince Horace.

_____ The girl who owns the bear and a man with a cart filled with potatoes are headed for the fair; the boys go with them.

_____ Prince Brat refuses to pretend to be a servant, so Jemmy sees no option but to run into the woods to escape from Hold-Your-Nose-Billy and Cutthroat. The prince follows.

_____ Prince Brat and Jemmy switch clothing.

_____ The bandits pursue the boys into the woods but are soon chased away by a trained bear.

_____ No longer pursued by the bandits, the boys leave the sewers; they learn that the king believes that Jemmy kidnapped the prince and that a reward is being offered for finding the prince.

_____ Prince Horace tells the potato man to collect the reward, and Prince Horace and Jemmy return to the palace.

_____ While at the fair Prince Horace overhears a lady talking about what a brat he is and he realizes that he does not want people to think of him in that way.

_____ Eventually they are found at the fair by the bandits and once again must flee; they run from the fair and head to the sewers.

_____ Wanting attention from the king, Prince Brat—now in Jemmy's clothing— runs away and takes Jemmy with him. Jemmy goes, hoping to go back to his life as a ratcatcher.

_____ Shortly after leaving the palace, the boys are kidnapped by Hold-Your-Nose-Billy and Cutthroat.

_____ Because Jemmy is wearing the prince's clothing and because he can read and do math, Hold-Your-Nose-Billy and Cutthroat think Jemmy is the prince.

_____ Because Jemmy was once a ratcatcher, he is very familiar with the sewers and is able to trick the bandits into entering a tunnel filled with rats.

_____ After being attacked by the rats, the bandits run from the sewers and give up their pursuit.

Sequence of Events:
Where in the Plot Is It?

Re-read the events of *The Whipping* in the order in which you numbered them. Then answer the following questions. You may refer to the event number rather than write them out.

1. Which event(s) belong to the section known as the exposition?

_____

2. Which event(s) could be labeled rising action?

_____

3. Which event represents the moment at which the conflict is most intense?

_____

4. How would you label the event described in the previous question?

_____

5. Which events are part of the falling action?

_____

6. What would be the proper label for Event #16?

_____

Conflict

Conflict is the struggle between two forces. It results when the main character, or protagonist, encounters a problem—a force which may prevent him or her from achieving a goal. There are four basic types of conflict, each involving a different type of obstacle.

Character Versus Character

The protagonist has a problem with one or more of the other characters.

Character Versus Self

The protagonist must deal with a problem within himself. The character has conflicting emotions that draw him in different directions.

Character Versus Society

The character has a problem with a particular segment of society: family, friends, community, rules, government, and so on.

Character Versus Nature

The character must deal with a force of nature.

NOTE: Some sources include a category for Character versus Fate; for example, when a character must deal with illness or disability. Others consider this part of Character versus Nature or Character versus Self, depending upon the situation.

EXAMPLE FROM LITERATURE

Number the Stars, by Lois Lowry
It is 1943 and ten-year-old Annemarie Johansen is living in Copenhagen, Denmark, with her parents and younger sister. Nazi soldiers have taken control. Her friend Ellen is Jewish, and like the other Jews in Denmark, she and her family are in danger of being taken from their homes.

Character Versus Character:
Annemarie has an encounter with the soldiers while delivering a secret package to her uncle.

Character Versus Self:
Annemarie has mixed feelings about hiding Ellen in their apartment. She wants to help but fears the soldiers.

Character Versus Society:
All of the main characters struggle against the imposed German rule.

Character Versus Nature:
Ellen's mother trips on a root and brakes her ankle.

Which Type of Conflict?

For each situation, decide which type of conflict it is. Circle the appropriate letter.

1. In *Stone Fox,* by John Reynolds Gardiner
Willy must find a way to pay the taxes owed by his grandfather to the government.

> A. Character Versus Character
> B. Character Versus Self
> C. Character Versus Society
> D. Character Versus Nature

2. In *Out of the Dust,* by Karen Hesse
Billie Jo and her family struggle to survive during the severe dust storms of the 1930s.

> A. Character Versus Character
> B. Character Versus Self
> C. Character Versus Society
> D. Character Versus Nature

3. In *The Door in the Wall,* by Marguerite de Angeli
Robin de Bureford is full of self-pity because of the illness that crippled his leg.

> A. Character Versus Character
> B. Character Versus Self
> C. Character Versus Society
> D. Character Versus Nature

4. In *Shiloh,* by Phyllis Reynolds Naylor
Marty wants to save Shiloh, the dog who has followed him home, from his cruel owner.

> A. Character Versus Character
> B. Character Versus Self
> C. Character Versus Society
> D. Character Versus Nature

5. In *Tuck Everlasting,* by Natalie Babbitt
The man in the yellow suit wants to tell the Tucks' secret and sell the magic water.

> A. Character Versus Character
> B. Character Versus Self
> C. Character Versus Society
> D. Character Versus Nature

Educational Books 'n' Bingo

Story Elements: Grades 3–6

Conflict Makes the Story!

Often it is the conflict in a story that makes it interesting. Think about books you have recently read. What problems or obstacles did the main character encounter? Find an example for each type of conflict. Identify the book and the author. Then describe the conflict.

Character Versus Character

Book and Author_____

Conflict: _____

_____

_____

Character Versus Self

Book and Author_____

Conflict: _____

_____

_____

Character Versus Society

Book and Author_____

Conflict: _____

_____

_____

Character Versus Nature

Book and Author_____

Conflict: _____

_____

_____

Create a Story Plot

Use this form to develop a story plot using the beginning given.

BEGINNING

EXPOSITION

I woke up and looked around. Next to my bed was a large suitcase, packed and ready to go. I walked over to the window and saw that the sun shone brightly and the sky was a beautiful shade of blue—not a cloud in the sky! By all accounts it appeared that it would be a great day to be taking my first airplane_____

_____

_____

MIDDLE

RISING ACTION

_____

_____

_____

_____

_____

_____

CLIMAX

_____

_____

FALLING ACTION

_____

_____

_____

END

RESOLUTION

_____

_____

Suspense

Suspense is the state of anxiety that results from the uncertainty of what will happen next in the story. All plots should have a certain amount of suspense or the reader will lose interest. Suspense builds when the fate of a character we care about is uncertain. It is greatest when the reader fears that there is a real possibility that something bad could happen to that character.

CREATING SUSPENSE

An author creates suspense by putting a character that we care about in danger. Sometimes the author gives the reader information the character does not have. In this case, the reader might feel tense or anxious even though the character does not. More often, the reader feels anxious because the character is anxious. A character—and, therefore, the reader—might feel anxious for many reasons. There are many things an author can use in a plot to add suspense. The following chart lists some of them.

Some Things That Add Suspense

- dangerous or mysterious people or things

- storms or other frightening settings

- suggestion or appearance of supernatural beings

- suggestion or appearance of monstrous creatures

- serious illness

- difficult decisions or unresolved issues

- unexpected occurrences

- vocabulary that instills fear

21

TECHNIQUES OF SUSPENSE

There are several techniques an author can use to intensify the suspense. Often the greatest suspense comes at the end of a chapter. When an author ends a chapter by hinting at something important about to happen, we call it a **cliffhanger.** Another technique is **foreshadowing,** or the planting of hints, throughout the story. Another important tool is **imagery.** Imagery appeals to the reader's senses—sight, sound, smell, touch, and taste—to help the reader form mental pictures. Careful **word choice** is also important. Choosing words with connotations that evoke fear or suspicion adds to the suspense.

EXAMPLES FROM LITERATURE:

Tuck Everlasting, by Natalie Babbitt (Chapter One)
SITUATION: The narrator has explained that the wood of Treegap is isolated because the cows are smart enough not to go there and that if the cows had gone there, things would be different.

"The people would have noticed the giant ash tree at the center of the wood, and then, in time, they'd have noticed the little spring bubbling up among its roots in spite of the pebbles piled there to conceal it. And that would have been a disaster so immense that this weary old earth owned or not to its fiery core, would have trembled on its axis like a beetle on a pin."

The above excerpt, which comes at the end of Chapter One, is a cliffhanger. The passage hints that there is something dangerous about the spring. Also, the use of vocabulary such as *disaster, fiery,* and *trembled* adds to the suspense.

The Tale of Despereaux, by Kate DiCamillo (Chapter 3, "Once Upon a Time")
SITUATION: Despereaux is reading a fairy tale from the princess's book.

"Despereaux did not know it, but he would need, very soon, to be brave himself."

The author uses foreshadowing to create suspense by telling us that he will have to be brave.

"Have I mentioned that beneath the castle there was a dungeon? In the dungeon, there were rats. Large rats. Mean rats. Despereaux was destined to meet those rats."

The suspense is intensified when we are told that there is a dungeon with large, mean rats and that Despereaux is destined to meet them.

Why Worry?

For each passage, explain the factor or factors responsible for the suspense. Use the following list to help you in your analysis.

Dangerous Opponent   Dangerous Thing or Place

Mysterious Stranger   Frightening Weather

Dark Setting   Supernatural or Monstrous Creature

Serious Illness   Imagery

1. From *Mrs. Frisby and the Rats of NIMH*, by Robert C. O'Brien (Chapter 1, "Mr. Ages")
SITUATION: Mrs. Frisby and her children cannot move to their summer home because Timothy is ill.
"And then, as if to make things worse, she heard a sound that filled her with alarm. It came from across the fence in the farmyard, a loud sputtering roar. It was Mr. Fitzgibbon starting his tractor."

_____

_____

_____

2. From *Number the Stars*, by Lois Lowry (Chapter 5, "Who Is the Dark-Haired One?)
SITUATION: The Johansens are hiding Ellen from the Nazis; they say she is their daughter.
"Annemarie looked around. These three uniformed men were different from the ones on the street corners. The street soldiers were often young, sometimes ill at ease. ... But these men were older and their faces were filled with anger."

_____

_____

_____

3. From *A Year Down Yonder,* by Richard Peck ("Gone with the Wind")
SITUATION: The sky has turned a shade of yellow Mary Alice has never seen.
"Then in the midst of an ideal day, the sky outside our classroom windows turned a shade of yellow I'd never seen. We were in Home Ec., and the room stirred. This was one of those times when everybody else knew something I didn't. The siren on the town water tower suddenly wailed. ... I was petrified. I'd heard about tornadoes, but thought they happened somewhere else."

_____

_____

_____

Foreshadowing

Foreshadowing is the technique authors use to hint at something that will happen or something we will learn later on in the book. There are two main reasons to use foreshadowing. The first is to build suspense. The second is to prepare readers for what will happen—either good or bad—and to make the story more believable. Sometimes, especially in mysteries, an author includes some misleading clues. These misleading clues are known as **red herrings**.

EXAMPLES FROM LITERATURE:

Tuck Everlasting, by Natalie Babbitt

Foreshadowing helps readers guess that the Tucks are immortal because of the spring water. The first excerpt hints of their immortality and the second leads us to believe the water is the cause.

"For Mae Tuck, and her husband, and Miles and Jesse, too had all looked the same for eighty-seven years." (Chapter 2)

In Chapter 5 Jesse tells Winnie that he is 104, but she thinks he is kidding. A short while later, she wants to drink from the spring from which he has taken a drink, but he stops her.

" 'Believe me, Winnie Foster,' said Jesse, 'it would be terrible for you if you drank any of this water.' "

Holes, by Louis Sacher

There are many examples of foreshadowing in this novel; many have to do with the mention of yellow-spotted lizards. These and other references to the yellow-spotted lizards foretell the fact that a main character will be in danger because of the lizards.

"But you don't want to be bitten by a yellow-spotted lizard. ... That's the worst thing that can happen to you." (Chapter 1)

"If you get bitten by a yellow-spotted lizard, you might as well go into the shade of the oak trees and lie in the hammock. There is nothing anyone can do for you anymore." (Chapter 1)

"The yellow-spotted lizards like to live in holes. ... Up to twenty lizards may live in one hole." (Chapter 8)

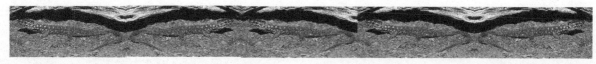

What Might That Mean?

For each excerpt, choose an event that it foreshadows.

        A. The Tucks' secret about immortality will be known.

        B. Her sister has a serious illness.

        C. The protagonist will be accused of witchcraft.

        D. The stranger will steal the rifle.

        E. The girls may be in danger due to the presence of the soldiers.

1. From *Kira-Kira*, by Cynthia Kadohota (Chapter 8)

" My mother hadn't said a word since we'd left home. I could tell that she was worried about Lynn. I knew that my father … was worried too. … The measles did not seem like such a horrible thing. … anemia was not so terrible either. … And yet my parents were very worried."

Foreshadows: _____   _____

2. From *Tuck Everlasting*, by Natalie Babbitt (Chapter 5)

Winnie Foster has met Jesse Tuck in the wood, and Jesse has brought her home. The Tucks are immortal; they cannot die. No one else knows. When Mae Tuck sees that Jesse has brought a girl to their home, she says, " 'Well, boys, here it is. The worst is happening at last.' "

Foreshadows: _____

3. From *Number the Stars*, by Lois Lowry (Chapter 1, "Why Are You Running?")

Annemarie Johansen, Ellen Rosen, and Annemarie's little sister Kirsti have been stopped by the German soldiers for running. Mrs. Rosen says, " 'I must go to speak to Ellen. You girls walk a different way to school tomorrow. Promise me, Annemarie. And Ellen will promise, too.' "

Foreshadows: _____

4. From *The Witch of Blackbird Pond*, by Elizabeth George Speare (Chapter 1)

Kit jumps into the water to save a child. Nat teases her by saying, " 'Don't you know about the water trial? 'Tis a sure test. … A true witch always floats. The innocent ones just sink like a stone.' "

Foreshadows: _____

5. From *Sign of the Beaver*, by Elizabeth George Speare (Chapter 2)

We are told that Matt "was not so quick-witted when unexpectedly someone arrived." The stranger notices the rifle that Matt's father had given him before leaving him on his own.

Foreshadows: _____

Flashback

Flashback is the technique authors use to tell readers about an event that happened before the current action of the story. The information should have something to do with the main part of the story.

EXAMPLES FROM LITERATURE:

Holes, by Louis Sachar

In *Holes,* the author uses flashback throughout the novel. One use of flashback in this novel is to tell **a story within the story.** The main plot is about Stanley Yelnats, who is wrongfully accused of theft and is sent to Camp Green Lake, which is really a boys' detention center. The author uses flashback to take the reader back generations; at the end the stories are tied together. Flashback is also used to explain how Stanley got to be in his present predicament.

Where the Red Fern Grows, by Wilson Rawls

Most of the novel is a flashback. The book is told in the first person. In the first chapter we learn that the narrator comes across an injured old redbone hound who reminds him of the dogs he had as a youngster. Most of the novel involves the retelling of the story about him and his dogs.

"Although he had no way of knowing it, he had stirred memories, and what priceless treasures they were. Memories of my boyhood days. ... Two beautiful cups gleamed from the mantel. ... I got up and took them down. There was a story in those cups — a story that went back more than a half century. As I caressed the smooth surfaces, my mind drifted back through the years, back to my boyhood days. How wonderful the memories were. Piece by piece the story unfolded."

Educational Books 'n' Bingo

Story Elements: Grades 3–6

Flashback: What Do We Learn?

For each example of flashback, identify the important information learned by readers.

1. From *The Sign of the Beaver,* by Elizabeth George Speare (Chapter 1)

"He knew it was high time his father was starting back. This was part of the plan that the family had worked out together in the long winter of 1766 … back in Massachusetts. … In the spring … Matt and his father would … take passage on a ship to the settlement at the mouth of the Penobscot River. … They would clear a patch of ground, build a cabin, and plant some corn. In the summer his father would go back to Massachusetts to fetch his mother and sister and the new baby. … Matt would stay behind and guard the cabin and the corn patch."

_____

_____

_____

_____

2. From *The Sign of the Beaver,* by Elizabeth George Speare (Chapter 1)

"Then, just before he left, his father had given him a second gift. … 'I'll take your old blunderbuss with me,' his father had said. 'This one aims truer. But mind you, don't go banging away at everything that moves. Wait till you're dead sure. There's plenty of powder if you don't waste it.' "

_____

_____

_____

3. From *Kira-Kira,* by Cynthia Kadohata (Chapter 1)

The entire first chapter is flashback. Here are a few excerpts:
"*Kira-kira* means 'glittering.' Lynn told me that when I was a baby we used to … lie on our backs and look at the stars while she said over and over, 'Katie, say *kira-kira, kira-kira.*' "
"I was born in Iowa in 1951. I know a lot about when I was a little girl, because my sister [Lynn] used to keep a diary. Today I keep her diary in a drawer next to my bed."
"A few weeks after [my father's] store went out of business, my father decided to take us down to Georgia to join the poultry industry."

_____

_____

_____

_____

Educational Books 'n' Bingo

Creating Flashback

Write a short story using flashback. Your flashback should provide the reader with information about the situation. Choose one of these story starters or use one of your own. Jot your ideas here and then write your story on another sheet of paper.

STORY STARTER #1: It was Saturday morning, but Liam was too excited to sleep late. Today was his birthday and his parents had told him that they had a special surprise for him. When he went into the living room, his mother handed him an envelope. As Liam opened the envelope, his father said, "As this year's birthday present, we have bought tickets to the circus for you and five of your friends." Liam was speechless! "Oh, no!" he thought. "Anywhere but the circus!" His mind drifted back to last year—

STORY STARTER #2: Emma stepped out of the wheelchair and hopped into the backseat of her father's car. It was difficult to get comfortable with that cast on her leg! Eight weeks the doctor had said! "What a way to spend summer vacation," she thought. To think, just yesterday she—

SITUATION #3: Lamont's Aunt Larita has invited him and his family to spend the week at their seaside home. If it were anywhere else Lamont would have been thrilled to learn that his parents had accepted the invitation. As he listened to his mother and father discuss all that they would do there, Lamont's mind went back two summers ago to the last time they went to the beach—

_____

_____

_____

_____

_____

_____

_____

_____

_____

_____

_____

_____

_____

_____

Character

Character is a very important literary element. A **character** is an imaginary person (or animal or fantasy being) created by the author. There are two basic types of characters: protagonists and antagonists. The main character is called the **protagonist.** (Most novels have one protagonist, but there may be more than one.) The character or force that opposes the protagonist is called the **antagonist.**

We describe characters as either static or dynamic and either flat or round. A **static character** stays pretty much the same throughout the work. A **dynamic character** changes in an important way. **Flat characters** are not fully developed; we see only one aspect of them. **Stereotypes**, characters with traits associated with a particular class, are flat characters. So are **stock characters**, or characters meant to represent an entire class of people. **Well-rounded** characters, on the other hand, are well developed; we see many traits—both good and bad. If a character is well developed, we almost feel as if we really know the person. Dynamic, round characters are usually the most interesting.

EXAMPLES FROM LITERATURE:

DYNAMIC CHARACTER
A Christmas Carol, by Charles Dickens
One of the best examples of a dynamic character is Ebenezer Scrooge, the protagonist of *A Christmas Carol.* At the start of the novel, Scrooge is a heartless miser who thinks only of his own well being; he keeps to himself and shows no emotion. Scrooge is visited by the Ghost of Christmas Past, the Ghost of Christmas Present, and Ghost of Christmas Yet to Come. With each visit, we see changes in Scrooge. By the end of the novel, he is a generous, caring, and loving man.

STATIC CHARACTER
Cinderella
Although dynamic characters are more interesting, characters in stories for young children are often static. By showing only one type of trait, it makes it easier for young readers to understand. In the story of Cinderella, for example, Cinderella is shown to be kind and generous. Her stepmother and stepsisters are shown to be cruel and selfish.

Character Traits

When describing a character, we use the term "character trait." **Character traits** are descriptive adjectives that tell us about a character's qualities. They are the same traits that could be used to describe a real person as well.

Brainstorm a list of character traits. See how many you can write. Think about characters in the books you have read. The list has been started for you.

1. *kind*
2. *cruel*

Follow-up Activities

1. Look at the list of traits on the following page. Look up the meanings of any unfamiliar words.
2. Do you have any that are not on the list? If so, insert them in the appropriate place.
3. Use the list of character traits to create analogies. EXAMPLE: good : bad :: kind : cruel
4. Categorize the traits as Positive, Negative, and Neutral. Not everyone will agree!
5. Use the traits to write an acrostic poem about someone.

Character Traits

able	disrespectful	impatient	religious
aggressive	dumb	inconsiderate	respectful
anxious	easy-going	independent	responsible
argumentative	empathetic	industrious	rude
arrogant	evil	innocent	sad
bad	extroverted	intelligent	self-centered
belligerent	faithful	kind	selfish
boastful	fastidious	lazy	serious
bossy	fearful	loving	shy
brave	foolhardy	loyal	smart
brilliant	foolish	mean	sneaky
careful	fresh	messy	spoiled
careless	friendly	mysterious	stingy
caring	fun-loving	naive	strong-willed
charismatic	funny	narcissistic	stubborn
charming	generous	naughty	supportive
childish	gentle	neat	sympathetic
cooperative	giving	nervous	thoughtful
courageous	good	nice	tricky
cowardly	gallant	obedient	trusting
creative	greedy	optimistic	trustworthy
cruel	grumpy	passive	uncooperative
curious	happy	patient	undependable
daring	hardworking	persevering	unreliable
demanding	hateful	pessimistic	unselfish
dependable	helpful	pleasant	vain
depressed	honest	polite	well-intentioned
determined	hopeful	proud	well-mannered
dishonest	humble	quick	wicked
disloyal	imaginative	quiet	wise
disobedient	immature	reliable	zealous

Write a Character Sketch

Choose a book you have recently read that has a character you found interesting. Write at least ten traits that would describe that character.

Name of Book: _____

Author: _____

Name of Character: _____

1.   6.

2.   7.

3.   8.

4.   9.

5.   10.

Use the above traits to write a character sketch.

_____

_____
_____
_____
_____
_____
_____
_____
_____
_____
_____
_____
_____
_____
_____
_____

Educational Books 'n' Bingo

Characterization

Characterization refers to the techniques an author uses to create and reveal the traits of the characters. Sometimes an author tells the readers directly about a character. Often, however, readers must make inferences. Some of the techniques authors use to develop a character are listed in the chart below.

MEANS OF CREATING AND DEVELOPING A CHARACTER

DIRECT: The author tells the readers about a character's traits directly through the use of a narrator.

INDIRECT: Readers must infer the character's traits:
- from what the character says,
- from what the character does,
- from what the character thinks,
- from how the character looks,
- from what other characters say about him or her,
- from how the other characters react to him or her, and
- from what the narrator tells us about the character.

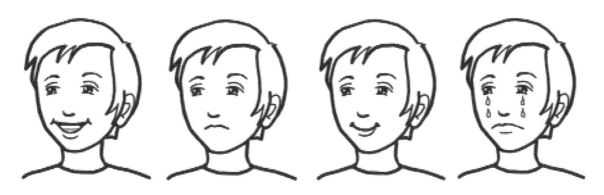

An Interesting Character

The following excerpts are from *A Long Way From Chicago,* by Richard Peck. The book describes seven summers Mary Alice and Joey Dowdel spend with their grandmother in southern Illinois. Outwardly, Grandma is a gruff, tough woman who does outrageous things. She often lies and breaks the law to achieve what she considers true justice. However, there are many other sides to Grandma Dowdel. Read each excerpt and explain how and what we learn about her.

1. Situation: Mary Alice and Joey drop into the Coffee Pot Cafe. (1929)
"The Coffee Pot was where people went to loaf, talk tall, and swap gossip. Mary Alice and I were of some interest when we dropped by because we were kin of Mrs. Dowdel's, who never set foot in the place. She said she liked to keep herself to herself, which was uphill work in a town like that."

_____

_____

2. Situation: The Cowgill brothers, whose family run the dairy, destroyed Grandma's mailbox and Effie Wilcox's privy. Grandma tricks Mr. Cowgill into thinking the boys put a mouse in her milk bottle so Mr. Cowgill would punish them. He had made light of their pranks, but Grandma knew he would care if he thought their actions would affect his business. (1930)
" 'Thugs like yours who prey on two old helpless widow women ... is liable to get up to anything. Many more mice in the milk, and your customers will start keeping their own cows again.' "

_____

_____

3. Situation: Grandma doesn't tell Aunt Puss that Mary Alice and Joey are her grandchildren. (1931)
Joey thinks, "I had a sudden thought. Aunt Puss thought Grandma, Mary Alice and I were all about the same age. She hadn't noticed the years passing. That's why Grandma didn't say we were her grandkids. It would just have mixed up Aunt Puss."

_____

_____

4. Situation: Grandma feeds Aunt Puss once a week. She also feeds the hungry drifters. (1931)
Mary Alice says, " 'You take her food every week, don't you, Grandma.' "
Grandma responds, " 'But it's private business between her and me.' "

"Grandma gave them good food and a beer to wet their whistles. ... They didn't say much. They didn't thank her. She wasn't looking for thanks."

_____

_____

Create a Character

You have been asked to create a character for a new TV series. Respond to the following in order to help you develop your character.

What is your character's gender? _____

What is your character's age? _____

What is your character's profession? _____

Is your character's profession important to the plot?

_____

_____

_____

Write a physical description of your character. Include his or her manner of dress.

_____

_____

_____

_____

_____

_____

What are your character's strengths?

_____

_____

_____

_____

What are your character's weaknesses?

_____

_____

_____

_____

Educational Books 'n' Bingo

Does your character have any fears or phobias?

_____

_____

Does your character use any special kinds of speech?

_____

_____

Does your character wear any special clothing or use any special equipment?

_____

_____

How would you describe his or her values?

_____

_____

How important are friends and family to your character?

_____

_____

_____

_____

What does your character hope to achieve?

_____

_____

_____

_____

Who or what stands in the way of your character's achieving his or her goal?

_____

_____

_____

_____

Create a Story

Use your filled-in Create-a-Character sheet to help you create a story plot with the character you created as the protagonist.

BEGINNING

EXPOSITION

_____

_____

_____

MIDDLE

RISING ACTION

_____

_____

_____

_____

_____

CLIMAX

_____

_____

FALLING ACTION

_____

_____

_____

_____

END

RESOLUTION

_____

_____

_____

Educational Books 'n' Bingo

Character #1 Meets Character #2

Copy your completed Create-a-Character sheets and exchange sheets with a classmate. Write a short story involving the two characters. Will they cooperate with one another, or will they conflict?

BEGINNING

EXPOSITION

_____

_____

_____

MIDDLE

RISING ACTION

_____

_____

_____

_____

_____

CLIMAX

_____

_____

FALLING ACTION

_____

_____

_____

END

RESOLUTION

_____

_____

_____

Setting

Setting refers to the time and location in which a story takes place. It includes scenery, weather, clothing, furniture, and other elements associated with the period of time and geographical location. It also includes the social and political environment. Some settings are general and some are specific. Setting can help set the mood, or atmosphere, of the story. It can also provide important background; this is especially important in historical fiction as shown in the examples below. Occasionally, setting is used to symbolize an important theme of the story. In some works of literature, the setting is an integral part of the story. In others, it is not as important.

EXAMPLES FROM LITERATURE:

The following are examples of novels whose settings are vital to the story. In all three examples, all elements of the story are influenced by the setting.

Out of the Dust, by Karen Hesse

Out of the Dust is set in Oklahoma from the winter of 1934 through the autumn of 1935. It takes place during the devastating dust storms and the Great Depression. Setting is essential to the plot and influences all the other elements of the novel. This story would make no sense if set in a different time and place.

Number the Stars, by Lois Lowry

Number the Stars is about a Danish family who helps their Jewish friends escape from the Nazis. The story must be set during this time period and in this location or there could be no story. In other words, the setting is such an integral part of the story that it cannot be changed. It would not make sense if set in a different time and place.

The Witch of Blackbird Pond, by Elizabeth George Speare

This novel is set in 1687 and 1688 in the Puritan settlement of Wethersfield in the Connecticut Colony. The people are deeply religious, dress simply, and work hard. Kit, the protagonist, who has recently arrived from Barbados, is accused by Goodwife Cruff of being a witch because she can swim. Kit befriends Hannah, who is called the Witch of Blackbird Pond by the townspeople because she is a Quaker. When an illness spreads through the town, many blame Hannah and they burn her house, hoping to kill her. The setting is very important to the story because the Puritans who settled in New England were not very tolerant of other people's views. During this time period, many—especially women—were accused of witchcraft.

===== 39 =====

Story Elements, Grades 3–6

Educational Books 'n' Bingo

Match the Excerpt and Setting

For each excerpt, choose the correct book and setting. Write the letter on the line.

A. *Heidi,* by Johanna Spyri; Setting: Swiss Alps

B. *Number the Stars,* by Lois Lowry; Setting: Denmark in 1943

C. *Anne of Green Gables,* by L. M. Montgomery; Setting: Prince Edward Island, Canada, early 1900s

D. *The Door in the Wall,* by Marguerite de Angeli; Setting: Medieval England

E. *Lily's Crossing,* by Patricia Reilly Giff; Setting: Rockaway, New York, during World War II

F. *The Witch of Blackbird Pond,* by Elizabeth George Speare; Setting: Connecticut Colony 1687–1688

_____ 1. " 'I'm not expecting a girl,' said Matthew blankly. 'It's a boy I've come for ... Mrs. Alexander Spencer was to bring him over from Nova Scotia for me.' "

_____ 2. "After climbing for about an hour, they came to the little village of Dörfli, halfway up the mountain."

_____ 3. "Ever since he could remember, Robin had been told what was expected of him as son of his father. Like other sons of noble family, he would be sent away from his mother and father to live in the household of another knight."

_____ 4. "And she know what Resistance meant. Papa had explained when she overheard the word and asked. Resistance fighters were Danish people—no one knew who, because they were very secret—who were determined to bring harm to the Nazis however they could."

_____ 5 "At least this grim place was not her destination, and surely the colony at Wethersfield would prove more inviting."

_____ 6. "Eddie at Normandy Beach on D-Day? Everyone had talked about it all through the war ... the day that the Allies ... would land in France."

Story Elements: Grades 3–6

A New Setting

Where a story is set can have a great impact on the plot, the characters, and the mood of the story. Choose one of the following and think about how it would change the story. Write a summary of the story using the new setting.

Suppose ...

Hansel and Gretel lived in New York City.

Snow White and the Seven Dwarfs lived in Hawaii.

The Three Bears lived in a mobile home.

Rapunzel was locked in a dungeon instead of a tower.

The Third Little Pig bought a condominium.

_____

_____

_____

_____

_____

_____

_____

_____

_____

_____

_____

_____

_____

_____

_____

_____

_____

_____

_____

_____

Point of View

Point of view has to do with who tells the story; in other words, who is the **narrator.** In a **first-person narration,** one of the characters is telling the story. The author uses the word "I" or "we" and their forms to refer to that character. The first-person narrator can be the protagonist, someone who is close to the protagonist, or a relatively unimportant character in the story. In a **third-person narration,** none of the characters is telling the story. The author uses the words "he," "she," "it," and "they" and their forms to refer to all of the characters. The third-person narrator can be either omniscient or limited. If the narrator tells us everything about the story, we say it is an omniscient, or all-knowing, narrator. An omniscient narrator tells us about the feelings, thoughts, and motives of all the characters. If the author tells us the story from the perspective of one of the characters, we say it is a limited third-person point of view. Sometimes an author uses a **second-person point of view**. In this case, the author speaks directly to the readers. This is more common in guides and handbooks than in literature.

EXAMPLES FROM LITERATURE:

FIRST-PERSON NARRATOR
The Lightning Thief, by Rick Riordan

This novel has a first-person narrator. The story is told from the perspective, or point of view, of Percy Jackson. The author uses words such as "I," "me," and "my" when referring to Percy. In the first chapter we are told, "My name is Percy Jackson. I'm twelve years old. Until a few months ago, I was a boarding student at Yancy Academy, a private school for troubled kids in upstate New York."

THIRD-PERSON NARRATOR
Flora & Ulysses, by Kate DiCamillo

This story is told by a third-person narrator. The author tells us about the characters. None of the characters acts as narrator. Flora and Ulysses, a squirrel who gains super powers following a potentially tragic accident, are the main characters.

Chapter One begins, "Flora Belle Buckman was in her room at her desk. She was very busy. She was doing two things at once. She was ignoring her mother, and she was also reading a comic book entitled *The Illuminated Adventures of the Amazing Incandesto!*"

Chapter Eleven begins, "She put Ulysses down on her bed, and he looked even smaller sitting there in the bright overhead light."

Whose Point of View?

Read each excerpt. Using only the information in the excerpt, decide whether the story is told from a first-person or third-person point of view. Write "first person" or "third person" on the top line. If it is a first-person narration, see if you can determine the character's name. If you can, write that name on the line. If it is a first-person narration but you cannot tell the character's name, write "unknown."

1. From *Moon Over Manifest,* by Clare Vanderpool (Chapter 1)

"I thought about my daddy, Gideon Tucker. ... On the occasion when he'd say to me, 'Abilene, did I tell you 'bout the time ...?' I'd get real quiet and listen real hard."

POINT OF VIEW: _____

CHARACTER'S NAME (If first-person narrator): _____

2. From *Because of Winn Dixie,* by Kate DiCamillo (Chapter One)

"My name is India Opal Buloni, and last summer my daddy, the preacher, sent me to the store ... and I came back with a dog."

POINT OF VIEW: _____

CHARACTER'S NAME (If first-person narrator): _____

3. From *Maniac Magee,* by Jerry Spinelli (Chapter 3)

"As for the first person to actually stop and talk with Maniac, that would be Amanda Beale. And it happened because of a mistake."

POINT OF VIEW: _____

CHARACTER'S NAME (If first-person narrator): _____

4. From *Charlie and the Chocolate Factory*, by Roald Dahl (Chapter 1)

"The whole of this family—the six grownups … and little Charlie Buckett—live together in a small wooden house on the edge of a great town."

POINT OF VIEW: _____

CHARACTER'S NAME (If first-person narrator): _____

5. From *Mrs. Frisby and the Rats of NIMH*, by Robert C. O'Brien (The Sickness of Timothy Frisby)

"Mrs. Frisby, the head of a family of field mice, lived in the vegetable garden of a farmer named Mr. Fitzgibbon."

POINT OF VIEW: _____

CHARACTER'S NAME (If first-person narrator): _____

6. From *Black Beauty*, by Anne Sewell (Chapter 1, "My Early Years")

"There were six young colts in the meadow besides me; they were older than I was; some were nearly as large as grown-up horses."

POINT OF VIEW: _____

CHARACTER'S NAME (If first-person narrator): _____

That Changes Everything!

Write a paragraph about one of the following—first from your point of view and then from the point of view of someone else involved in the incident.

An Argument You Had with Someone

A Contest You Won (or Lost)

An Embarrassing Moment for You

Your Favorite Team Wins (or Loses)

You Think Someone Has Stolen Your Favorite _____

My Point of View

_____

_____

_____

_____

_____

_____

_____*'s Point of View*

_____

_____

_____

_____

_____

_____

How did changing the point of view change the story?

_____

_____

Tone and Mood

Tone and mood are similar, but they are not the same. The **tone** is the author's attitude toward the writing and the readers. For example, the tone might be serious or lighthearted. Setting, choice of vocabulary, and other details help set the tone, and a book can have more than one tone.

The **mood** is the general atmosphere created by the author's words. It is the feeling the reader gets from reading those words. It may stay the same, or it may change from situation to situation.

Some Words That May Be Used to Describe the Tone of a Book

Amused

Angry

Cheerful

Horror

Clear

Formal

Gloomy

Humorous

Informal

Ironic

Light

Matter-of-Fact

Resigned

Optimistic

Pessimistic

Playful

Pompous

Sad

Serious

Suspicious

Witty

Some Words That May Be Used to Describe the Mood of a Book

Fanciful

Frightening

Frustrating

Gloomy

Happy

Joyful

Melancholy

Mysterious

Romantic

Sentimental

Sorrowful

Suspenseful

A EXAMPLE FROM LITERATURE:

A Year Down Yonder, by Richard Peck
TONE
Often the tone of a book can be described in more than one way. The novel *A Year Down Yonder* is an example. The tone in the beginning is serious. The reason that Mary Alice is on her way to her grandmother's house is that it is the Depression and Mary Alice's father has lost his job. Her parents must move into a small apartment and there is no room for Mary Alice. However, the overall tone of the novel is lighthearted and humorous, due expecially to the humorous situations. It can also be described as informal; factors that contribute to this are the use of dialect; idioms; and figurative language, especially hyperbole.

MOOD
The mood of *A Year Down Yonder* varies. Here are some passages that evoke different moods:
FEARFUL: "Then I heard a scream. A scream too human, from down in the dipping corner of the field that the moon missed. An answering scream froze in my throat."
HAPPY: "She'd made me a halo so Carleen Lovejoy in all her tinsel wouldn't 'outshine' me. ... I'd have come dangerously close to kissing Grandma then, if she'd let me."
SAD: " 'Her boy was gassed in the trenches,' Grandma said, 'And shot up ... He gets a check from the government, but it don't keep them.' "
CONTENTMENT: "I was married in Grandma's house, in the front room. It was a sunny day in warm weather. ... We lived happily ever after."

Identifying Tone and Mood

Select a book you have recently read. Describe the tone and mood of the book. Find excerpts that help establish the tone and mood.

Book: _____ Author_____

_____

_____

_____

_____

_____

_____

_____

_____

_____

Educational Books 'n' Bingo

Style

Every author has a particular **style** of writing, but he or she may vary that style depending upon the subject matter, the audience, and other factors. Style includes such factors as the use of dialect and/or dialogue, word choice, sentence length, grammatical structures, the use of imagery and figurative language, and the use of humor.

EXAMPLE FROM LITERATURE:

Flora and Ulysses, by Kate DiCamillo

The story is told from a third-person point of view. In general the style is characterized by matter-of-fact descriptions, short paragraphs, short chapters, and the occasional use of comic strips. Language is important to the protagonists and, therefore, the author uses interesting vocabulary, good sentence structure, and good grammar in both the narration and the dialogue. The mood varies, but in spite of some sad aspects to the story, the humorous tone dominates. We never really worry about what will happen to the main characters.

Flora is a well-rounded character. She says she is a cynic (someone who believes all or most people have selfish motives), but she is quick to act and be helpful when someone (or some squirrel) is in trouble. Language is very important to her; she is especially fond of the word *malfeasance* because she wants to rid the world of it! She is also a dynamic character. At first she is not anxious to befriend William Spiver, but she and he become good friends. Through most of the novel she thinks her mother does not love her, but by the end she realizes that she does. She also changes from a cynic to a much more optimistic character.

The author uses some figurative language and devices of sound but not often. However, many of her descriptions do contain imagery. The following is an example; it describes what Ulysses (the squirrel who now has super powers) sees as he looks around the room in Flora's house; the images in this passage appeal to our sense of sight: "He looked around the room. There was a **tall window**, and outside the window was the **green, green world** and the **blue sky.** Inside, there were **shelves of books.** And on the wall above the keyboard there was a picture of a man and woman **floating** over a city. They were suspended in a **golden light**. ...."

The author uses flashback a few times. For example, in the beginning Flora recalls the contract she had signed with her mother, an author of romance novels. In it she had agreed to read fewer comic books and more "true literature." The author also refers back to before Flora's parents were divorced. "Flora's father had said, 'I think that your mother is so in love with her books about love that she doesn't love me anymore.' "

Elements of Style

Sentence Structure
Long or short?
Many subordinate clauses?
Straightforward?
Unusual word order?

Paragraph Structure
Descriptive?
Action based?

Choice of Vocabulary
Interesting words?
Unusual or difficult vocabulary?
Regional expressions?

Dialogue
How often?
How important?
Natural?

Point of View
First-person narrator?
Third-person narrator?

Characterization
Dynamic characters?
Well-rounded characters?
Stereotypes?
Stock characters?

Tone and Mood

Use of Imagery

Use of Figurative Language

Use of Devices of Sound

Use of Humor

Use of Foreshadowing and Suspense

Use of Flashback

Analyzing Style

Choose a book you have read recently and analyze the author's style. Use the Elements of Style chart to help you. Address as many of the elements as possible.

Book: _____ Author_____

_____
_____
_____
_____
_____
_____
_____
_____
_____
_____
_____
_____
_____
_____
_____
_____
_____
_____
_____
_____
_____
_____
_____
_____
_____

Theme

Theme is the general idea or point of a story. It provides a basic message about life. The theme is different from the subject of the story. The subject is the topic on which the story is based. The theme is the author's expressed or implied opinion about that subject. For example, suppose an author writes about a family stranded on a desert island. The family is the subject of the story. The theme, however, might be the *importance* of family. Most works of fiction have at least one theme and may have more than one. On the other hand, it may have none at all.

An author can express his or her views in several ways. When trying to determine the theme of a story, think about other elements, such as character, plot, setting, and mood.

Questions to Ask Yourself to Help You Determine the Theme

How does the character change?

What makes him or her change?

What lessons does the character learn?

What are the characters' feelings about things that happen?

What kinds of conflicts are described?

How are the conflicts resolved?

Does any of the dialogue help convey the theme?

What mood does the author create?

COMMON THEMES

A theme cannot really be described in one word! For example, suppose you were told that the theme of a particular book is "friendship." There are many different themes that could be based upon friendship—some of them, such as the following two examples, are contradictory.

You can always count on your friends for emotional support.

The idea of having friends is overvalued.

The following are some common subjects for themes. Remember, however, that a theme should always be expressed in a complete sentence that expresses the author's point of view!

FRIENDSHIP	EDUCATION
SURVIVAL	MOTHERHOOD / FATHERHOOD
FAMILY	POVERTY / WEALTH
LOVE / HATE	PREJUDICE
LIFE / DEATH	LAWS / JUSTICE
FREEDOM	HONESTY
WAR / PEACE	HOMELESSNESS
PATRIOTISM	LAND

EXAMPLE FROM LITERATURE:

Tuck Everlasting, by Natalie Babbitt

There are several themes. One is the importance of maintaining the circle of life: birth, life, and death. If no one died, the world would suffer greatly. The Tucks have been doomed to eternal life. "Everything's a wheel, turning and turning, never stopping. The frogs is part of it, and the bugs, and the fish, and the wood thrush, too. And people. But never the same ones. Always coming in new, always growing and changing, and always moving on. ... That's the way it's supposed to be. That's the way it *is*."

Amos Fortune, Free Man, by Elizabeth Yates

The central theme of this book is the importance of freedom. It is clearly stated throughout the book. In the fourth chapter, "Woborn 1740–1779," Mrs. Richardson says to her husband, " 'Until they're given their freedom they count no more than cattle.' "

Life Lessons

For each excerpt, choose the most appropriate theme. Write the letter on the line.

THEMES:

A. Reading is a source of knowledge and power.

B. You should forgive those you love who have wronged you if they are truly sorry for what they have done.

C. Sometimes people must forget their differences and work together for the common good.

D. Bravery is doing what you know is right even when you are frightened.

E. You feel less lonely if you have someone to talk to who understands you.

EXCERPTS:

_____ 1. "Winn Dixie looked straight at me when I said that to him, like he was feeling relieved to finally have somebody understand his situation."
Because of Winn Dixie, by Kate DiCamillo (Chapter 3)

_____ 2. " 'By teaching us to read, they had taught us how to get away.' "
Mrs. Frisby and the Rats of NIMH, by Robert C. O'Brien ("The Air Ducts")

_____ 3. "These people in Shady's bar thought they knew little of each other as they hunkered with their own kind. ... But with the Hungarian woman's words, they suddenly recognized something in each other. They shared the same blood. Immigrant blood. ..."
" 'She's right. They've pushed us 'round long enough. ' "
"There was a solidarity among the people in Shady's bar that night, as one by one they emerged from their trenches and ventured into no-man's-land."
Moon Over Manifest, by Clare Vanderpool ("No-Man's-Land, July 20, 1918")

_____ 4. " 'I will tell you just a little because you were so very brave.' "
" 'Brave,' Annemarie asked, surprised. 'No, I wasn't. I was very frightened.' "
Number the Stars, by Lois Lowry (Chapter 16, "I Will Tell You Just a Little)

_____ 5. "Here are the words Despereaux Tilling spoke to his father. He said, 'I forgive you, Pa!' And he said these words because he sensed that it was the only way to save his heart, to stop it from breaking in two."
The Tale of Despereaux, by Kate DiCamillo (Chapter Forty, "Forgiveness")

Proverbs as Themes

One theme of *Walk Two Moons,* by Sharon Creech, is suggested by the title: the importance of empathy—the ability to understand and share another's feelings—as a source of understanding. The first message Phoebe finds on her porch states it directly: "Don't judge a man until you've walked two moons in his moccasins."

Brainstorm a list of proverbs and adages. The list has been started for you.

PROVERBS

Before you criticize a man, walk a mile in his shoes.

A penny saved is a penny earned.

Look before you leap.

Proverbs as Themes: Create a Story

Choose one of your proverbs as a theme for a story. Summarize the story. Then write a dialogue between two of the characters to express that theme.

SUMMARY OF STORY

_____

_____

_____

_____

_____

_____

_____

_____

_____

_____

_____

_____

_____

_____

DIALOGUE BETWEEN _____ **AND** _____

_____

_____

_____

_____

_____

_____

_____

_____

_____

_____

_____

_____

_____

_____

Story Elements, Grades 3–6   Educational Books 'n' Bingo

Literary Genres

Literature can be divided into classifications called **genres**. The two main classifications are non-fiction and fiction. Each may be further divided. A few genres of non-fiction are biographies, autobiographies, essays, and persuasive writings. The three main sub-genres of fiction are drama, which is written to be performed in front of an audience; poetry, which is often read aloud; and prose, which is usually read silently. Each of these, of course, can be further divided into more specific genres. Two main divisions of drama are comedy and tragedy. Two of the many genres of poetry are sonnet and ballad. Examples of genres of prose fiction include adventure novel, historical fiction, and science fiction.

GENRES OF PROSE FICTION

Genres of prose fiction are based upon subject matter, theme, tone, and the usage of literary devices and techniques. Often the categories overlap, and a book may fall into more than one classification.

The following are some genres with examples from classic and modern literature.

GENRE	EXAMPLE
ADVENTURE NOVEL	*Harry Potter and the Sorcerer's Stone,* by J.K. Rowling
FOLKLORE	*Aesop's Fables,* by Aesop
FANTASY	*A Wrinkle in Time,* by Madeleine L'Engle
HISTORICAL FICTION	*Number the Stars,* by Lois Lowry
HORROR	*Dracula,* by Bram Stoker
MYSTERY	Encyclopedia Brown Series, by Donald J. Sobol
REALISTIC FICTION	*Tales of a Fourth Grade Nothing,* by Judy Blume
SCIENCE FICTION	*When You Reach Me,* by Rebecca Stead

Which Genre Is It?

Read the descriptions on the next page. Choose a book you are reading or have recently read. Tell to which genre or genres it belongs and why. Cite examples to support your opinion.

_____

_____

_____

_____

_____

Popular Genres of Fiction Prose

There are many genres of fiction. These are a few of the more popular ones. Remember, many works of literature fit into more than one genre.

Adventure Novel

In this genre the protagonist has exciting adventures, putting himself in danger. The adventures are more important than in other genres.

Fantasy

Fantasy includes magic and supernatural occurrences as an integral part of the work.

Folktale

Folktales are stories that have been passed down from generation to generation. Fables, which feature animals and contain a moral; fairy tales, which have elves, fairies, and other such beings; myths, which explain the world view of a people and are associated with their religion or philosophy; and tall tales, which are exaggerated accounts of real or fictional events, are all types of folktales.

Historical Fiction

Historical fiction is set in a time period that occurred before the time of its writing. Although the story plot and some or all of the characters are fictional, the period is represented accurately.

Horror

Horror fiction includes elements of suspense, supernatural occurrences, and other factors that evoke terror. Their purpose was to instill terror; however, they emphasized elements of the supernatural and unknown.

Mystery

Mystery fiction requires the protagonist to figure out the details of a suspenseful event. Usually, that event is a crime. Crime fiction and detective fiction are sub-categories of this genre.

Realistic Fiction

Realistic fiction is set in contemporary times. Although the characters are fictional, the situations seem possible and the problems real.

Science Fiction

Science fiction relies, in part at least, on real or imagined science. It may or may not include time and/or space travel.

Which Genre?

For each description, decide how you would classify the work. Write the genres in the space to the left of each description. You may use more than one genre for a title, but you must use each genre at least once.

adventure **biography** **fantasy** **folktale** **historical fiction**
horror **mystery** **realistic fiction** **science fiction**

1. *Amos Fortune, Free Man,* by Elizabeth Yates
   This is the true story of Amos Fortune (1710 to 1801). Born a prince in Africa, he was captured and brought to the United States as a slave. He worked and saved to earn freedom for himself and others.

2. *The Lightning Thief,* by Rick Riordan
   Percy and his friends are on a quest to find and return Zeus's stolen lightning bolt. During their quest, they battle vicious monsters; are tricked by Ares, the god of war; and are almost stretched to death.

3. *The Westing Game,* by Ellen Raskin
   The of reading Sam Westing's will reveals that Westing was murdered by one of the heirs. The heirs are divided into teams and given clues to solve the murder, along with $10,000. The winner will inherit Westing's estate.

4. *A Wrinkle in Time,* by Madeleine L'Engle
   Meg, Calvin, and Charles are transported by supernatural beings as they search for Meg's father, who has been kidnapped and taken to another planet. They travel through time and space by means of a tesseract, a wrinkle in time.

5. *Coraline,* by Neil Gaiman
   Coraline ventures into a world that is eerily similar to her own. Other Mother at first resembles her mother but has black buttons instead of eyes. When Other Mother kidnaps her real parents, Coraline must rescue them and the souls of three ghost children or she will have to stay with Other Mother forever.

6. *Number the Stars,* by Lois Lowry
   The Rosens must go into hiding or risk being relocated by the Nazis. Ellen stays with her friend Annemarie and her family; she pretends to be Annemarie's sister.

7. *Tales of a Fourth Grade Nothing,* by Judy Blume
   Peter is fed up with the antics of his younger brother, Fudge, who gets away with everything.

8. *Johnny Appleseed,* by Steven Kellogg
   This is the larger-than-life story of John Chapman, better known as Johnny Appleseed.

9. *The Time Machine,* by H.G Wells
   The protagonist builds a time machine and travels into the future.

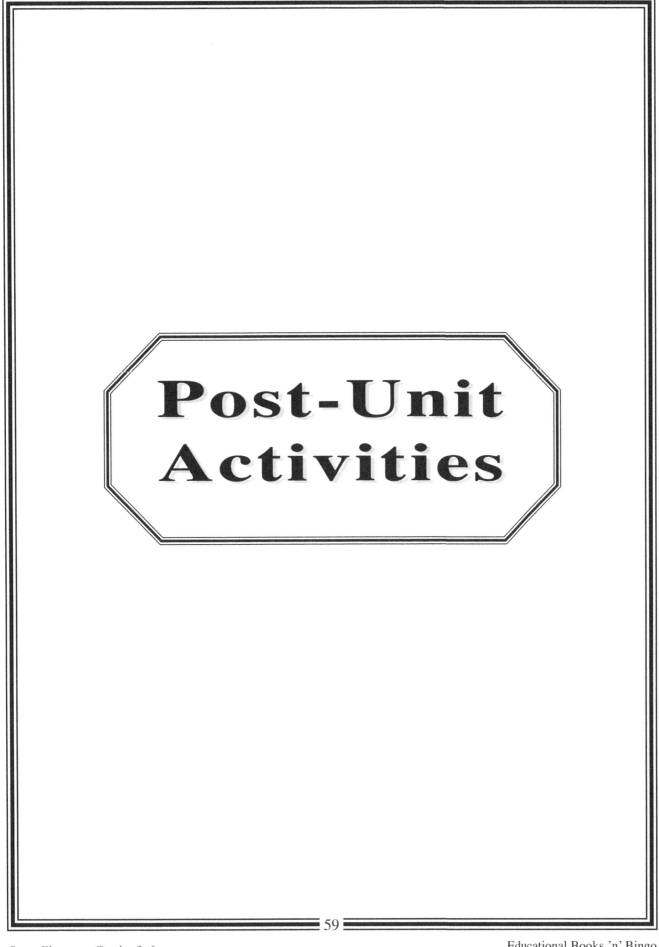

Post-Unit Activities

Post-Unit Activity
COMPARE AND CONTRAST

Choose two characters from a novel you have read. List as many character traits for each as you can. Then compare and contrast the two characters in a Venn diagram using the list of traits you compiled.

Name of Book: _____

Name of Author: _____

Character No. 1: _____ Character No. 2: _____

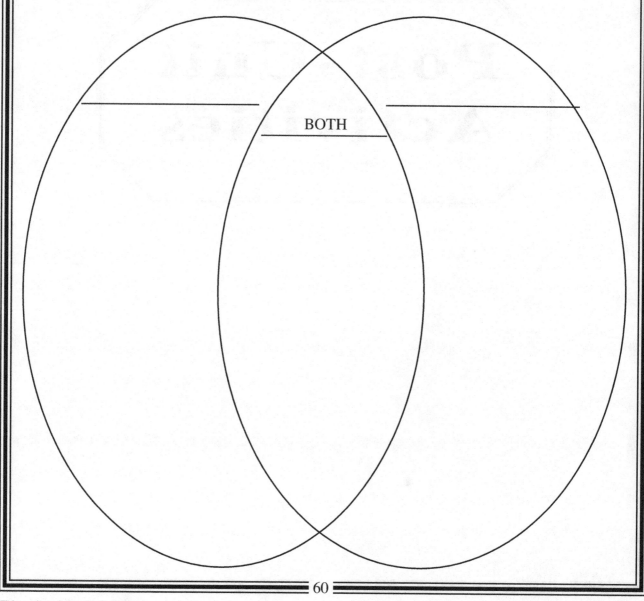

BOTH

Educational Books 'n' Bingo

Story Elements: Grades 3–6

Post-Unit Activity
ANOTHER POINT OF VIEW

Choose a well-known fairy tale and rewrite it from another character's point of view.

Name of Fairy Tale: _____

Character From Whose Point of View Original Tale Was Told:

_____

Character From Whose Point of View Your New Tale Will Be Told:

_____

_____

_____

_____

_____

_____

_____

_____

_____

_____

_____

_____

_____

_____

_____

_____

_____

_____

_____

_____

_____

_____

_____

Educational Books 'n' Bingo

Post-Unit Activity
A DYNAMIC CHARACTER

Choose a novel with a dynamic character. Tell how that character changed during the course of the story. Cite examples. You may use the form found on page 72.

Name of Book: _____

Name of Author: _____

Name of Character: _____

Brief Summary of Book

_____

_____

_____

_____

_____

How the Character Changed:

_____

_____

_____

_____

_____

_____

_____

_____

_____

_____

_____

_____

_____

_____

_____

_____

More Post-Unit Activities

Compare and contrast two books by different authors with a similar theme, setting, or plot.

Compare and contrast the tone of two books written by the same author.

Write a book review of a novel you recently read. Include information about the setting, characters, plot, theme, and style. Tell why you did or did not like the book.

Choose a fairy tale or other story. Show how one event leads to another.

List at least five character traits you might include in your autobiography.

Create Cause-and-Effect Sentences. Write five effects on a sheet of paper and exchange papers with a classmate. For each "effect" write a "cause" that might have led to it.

Judge the importance of setting in a book you are now reading or have recently read. Give reasons to support your opinion.

Find examples of good dialogue in a book you enjoyed reading. Explain why the dialogue was effective.

Choose a novel you have read that does not have chapter titles. Create chapter titles that foreshadow events and/or add suspense.

Create a word search puzzle using story elements and literary terms.

Research the origins of the term "cliffhanger" and evaluate the term.

Write five synonyms for the word "foreshadow."

Create a list of poetry genres.

Create an analogy using at least two literary elements.

Most fairy tale characters are flat. Write a short story that shows another side of a popular fairy-tale or folktale character.

Create an analogy that has to do with point of view.

Story Elements Crossword

ACROSS

3. ___action comes after the climax.
5. A ___-person narration is not told from a character's point of view.
7. The ordered sequence of causal events.
8. A conversation between two or more people.
12. A ___-person narration is told from a character's point of view.
14. The one who tells the story.
16. Referring to an event that occurred before a current event.
19. The main character in a story.
20. A synonym for "characteristic."
22. A category of literature; historical fiction is one.
23. The general atmosphere created by the author.

DOWN

1. A character who does not change.
2. A ___ character changes during the story.
4. The point in the story where the tension is greatest.
6. The struggle between two or more forces.
9. The end of the story where the conflict is resolved.
10. To use clues to hint at a future event.
11. An object that stands for an idea.
13. An author's manner of writing.
15. The opponent of the protagonist.
17. Where and when a story takes place.
18. The author's attitude toward the work.
20. A message the author wants to convey.
21. This word is used by a first-person narrator.

Story Elements Review

Choose from the list in the box to correctly complete each statement. Write your answers on the lines that come before each statement. Not all of the terms will be used.

characterization	first-person	point of view	style
chronological	flashback	protagonist	suspense
cliffhanger	flat	proverb	symbol
climax	foreshadowing	resolution	theme
conflict	genres	round	third-person
dynamic	mood	setting	tone
exposition	plot	static	trait

_____ 1. Apprehension or anxiety that results from the uncertainty of what will happen next is _____.

_____ 2. The part of the plot in which the setting is described and the main characters are introduced is the _____.

_____ 3. The moment in a story at which the conflict is most intense is called the _____.

_____ 4. _____ is the technique of telling readers something that happened in the past.

_____ 5. _____ hints at events yet to occur in a story.

_____ 6. _____ is the sequence of causal events in a story.

_____ 7. _____ describes most narrative order.

_____ 8. _____ is the struggle between two forces; it is present in all plots and occurs when the protagonist encounters a problem.

_____ 9. If a chapter ends in a suspenseful way, it is called a(n) _____.

_____ 10. Another word for the main character is _____.

_____ 11. A character who changes in an important way during the course of the story is said to be _____.

_____ 12. If a character is well developed, we say that character is _____.

_____ 13. The techniques an author uses to create and reveal the traits of the characters is called _____.

_____ 14. _____ refers to the period of time and the location of a story.

_____ 15. The author uses "I" to refer to one of the characters if the narration is from a(n) _____ point of view.

_____ 16. _____ is the general atmosphere created by the author's words.

_____ 17. _____ is the author's attitude toward the writing.

_____ 18. The author's use of vocabulary, grammar, sentence structure, imagery, and figurative language affects his or her _____.

_____ 19. _____ is the general message the author is trying to convey.

_____ 20. Literature is classified into divisions called _____.

_____ 21. A character who does not change is said to be _____.

_____ 22. An object that stands for an abstract idea is a(n) _____.

_____ 23. If a character is not well developed, we call it a(n) _____ character.

_____ 24. A personal characteristic, or quality, is called a character _____.

_____ 25. The _____ comes at the end of the story and ties up loose ends.

Educational Books 'n' Bingo

Story Elements: Grades 3–6

Appendix

Literary Elements

Literary elements, also known as Story Elements, are elements that apply to most works of literature. If you analyze any story, you are apt to find a plot, a setting, and a theme. You will also find one or more characters, and the story will be told from the point of view of one of those characters or from the point of view of a third-person narrator.

Plot and Conflict

Character

Setting

Point of View

Tone, Mood, and Style

Theme

Story Elements Chart

Name of Book: _____ Genre: _____

Author of Book: _____

CHARACTERS: Who are the main and secondary characters?

TRAITS OF MAIN CHARACTER(S):

PLOT

BEGINNING	MIDDLE	END

SETTING: When and where does story take place?

Character Development Chart

Use this chart to help you create a main character.

Name: _____ Age: _____

Occupation: _____

Likes and Dislikes	Goal(s)	Strengths and Weaknesses

Likes: _____ _____ Strengths: _____

_____ _____ _____

_____ _____ _____

_____ _____ _____

_____ _____ _____

_____ _____ _____

_____ _____ _____

Dislikes: _____ _____ Weaknesses: _____

_____ _____ _____

_____ _____ _____

_____ _____ _____

_____ _____ _____

_____ _____ _____

_____ _____ _____

_____ _____ _____

Glossary of Literary Terms

Alliteration: The repetition of initial consonant sounds in two or more consecutive or neighboring words.

Allusion: A reference to something outside the work in which it is found.

Antagonist: The opponent of the main character, or protagonist.

Anthropomorphism: When animals or inanimate objects are portrayed as people.

Character: An imaginary person in a work of fiction.

Character development: The method used by an author to develop a character.

Character trait: A distinguishing characteristic, or quality, of a character.

Characterization: The method used by the author to give readers information about a character; a description or representation of a person's qualities or peculiarities.

Climax: The moment in a story when the action reaches its greatest conflict.

Conflict: The struggle within a character, between characters, between a character and society, or between a character and a force of nature.

Connotation: The associations that are suggested or implied by a word that go beyond its dictionary meaning.

Denotation: The dictionary meaning of a word.

Denouement: The part of the plot where the main dramatic conflict is worked out; the plot may or may not have a happy ending. (Also called resolution.)

Dialect: A variety of a language that is distinguished from the standard form by pronunciation, grammar, and/or vocabulary.

Dialogue (dialog): Conversation between two or more characters.

Exposition: The beginning of a work of fiction; the part in which readers are given important background information.

Falling action: The action that comes after the climax and before the resolution.

Figurative language: Description of one thing in terms usually used for something else. Simile and metaphor are examples of figurative language.

Flashback: Insertion of an earlier event into the normal chronological sequence of a narrative.

Foil: A character with traits opposite to those of the main character.

Foreshadowing: The use of clues to give readers a hint of events yet to occur.

Genre: A category of literature.

Historical fiction: Fiction represented in a setting true to the history of the time in which the story takes place.

Hyperbole: An exaggeration used for effect.

Idiom: An expression whose meaning cannot be determined by its literal expression.

Image: A mental picture.

Imagery: The use of language that appeals to the senses and produces mental images; the use of figures of speech or vivid descriptions to produce mental images.

Irony (situational): An outcome contrary to what was or might have been expected.

Irony (verbal): The use of words to express the opposite of their literal meaning.

Metaphor: A figure of speech that compares two unlike things without the use of *like* or *as*.

Mood: The feeling that the author creates for the reader.

Narrator: The voice and implied speaker who tells the story.

Onomatopoeia: The use of words that mimic the sounds they represent.

Oxymoron: A figure of speech made up of seemingly contradictory parts.

Paradox: A statement or situation that seems contradictory but reveals a truth.

Personification: The bestowing of human qualities on inanimate objects, ideas, or animals. (See the difference between personification and anthropomorphism.)

Plot: The ordered structure, or sequence, of causal events in a story.

Point of view: The perspective from which a story is told; the relation of the narrator to the story.

Protagonist: The main character.

Pun: A humorous play on words that are similar in sound but different in meaning.

Realistic fiction: True-to-life fiction; people, places, and happenings are similar to those in real life.

Resolution: The part of the plot where the main dramatic conflict is worked out; the plot may or may not have a happy ending. (Also called denouement.)

Rising action: Events in a plot that occur after the exposition but before the climax.

Sarcasm: A form of verbal irony in which a person says the opposite of what he or she means.

Satire: A literary work that pokes fun at individual or societal weaknesses.

Sequencing: The placement of Story Elements: Grades 3–6 in a narrative order, usually chronological.

Setting: The time and place in which the main story events occur.

Simile: A figure of speech that clearly compares two unlike things through the use of *like* or *as*.

Stereotype: A character whose personality traits represent a group rather than an individual.

Style: The author's manner of writing, including grammatical structures, type of vocabulary, and the use of figurative language and other literary techniques.

Suspense: Quality that causes readers to wonder what will happen next; apprehension about what will happen.

Symbolism: The use of an object, character, or idea to represent something else.

Theme: The main idea of a literary work; the message the author wants to convey.

Tone: The attitude of the author towards his or her writing.

Understatement: To state something less strongly than the facts would indicate.

Answers

Cause and Effect (Page 14):
1. C 2. F 3. A 4. H 5. B 6. D 7. G 8. E

Sequence of Events: *The Prince and the Pauper* (Page 15):
The events should be numbered as follows: 16, 1, 6, 9, 7, 2, 8, 14, 15, 10, 11, 3, 4, 5, 12, 13.

Where in the Plot Is It?(Page 16):
1. The first three events belong to the exposition.
2. Events 4 through 9 could be labeled "rising action."
3. Event #10, when Prince Brat realizes that he does not want to be known as a brat, is most intense.
4. Event #10 would be called the climax.
5. Events 11 through 15 are falling action.
6. Event #16 could be labeled "resolution" or "denouement."

Which Type of Conflict? (Page 18):
1. C 2. D 3. B 4. A 5. A

Why Worry?(Page 23):
1. The setting is dangerous; there is a dangerous character; and there is serious illness. The mice are in their winter home and must leave before they are harmed by the tractor or by Mr. Fitzgibbon. Timothy is too ill to move. The excerpt is particularly suspenseful because Mrs. Frisby hears the sound of the tractor.
2. The Nazi soldiers are dangerous opponents. The fact that their faces are "filled with anger" makes it more suspenseful.
3. This passage is suspenseful because we know that a tornado is approaching. It is more suspenseful because we empathize with the first-person narrator, who is "petrified."

What Might That Mean? (Page 25):
1. B 2. A 3. E 4. C 5. D

Flashback (Page 27):
1. We learn that the setting is the summer of 1767 in a new settlement near the mouth of the Penobscot River. (We are not told in the passage, but the Penobscot River is in Maine.) We know that his father had returned to their old home in Massachusetts Colony to get Matt's mother, sister, and the new baby and that Matt had expected them to arrive at their new cabin by the time the story begins.
2. We can infer that his father was at least a little worried about leaving Matt there alone to guard the cabin. He gave Matt his rifle, which was better than Matt's blunderbuss, an old-fashioned gun with a wide opening at the end.
3. We learn the meaning of the title of the book. We learn that the first-person narrator was born in Iowa but that the story takes place in Georgia. That person seems to be very fond of her sister. We cannot be sure, but we may infer that her sister has died because it would be unusual for her to keep her sister's diary in a drawer next to her bed if her sister were still alive. We also know that her father worked (and may still work) in the poultry industry.

An Interesting Character (Page 34):

1. The author tells the reader through Joey, the first-person narrator, that Grandma did not like to socialize and gossip with the others.

2. We know through her words and actions that Grandma would lie and use trickery to get what she perceived as justice. We also learn that she is resourceful. Unfortunately, we also learn that she was not above harming the mouse to achieve her goal.

3. The author implies through her words and actions that deep down Grandma is a thoughtful, caring, compassionate person. She did not want to confuse Aunt Puss by saying that Mary Alice and Joey were her grandchildren.

4. Readers see again by her words and actions that Grandma is a caring person. They also learn that she does not care about the recognition of others. She helps these people without wanting anything in return.

Match the Excerpt and Setting (Page 40):
1. C   2. A   3. D   4. B   5. F   6. E

Whose Point of View? (Pages 43–44):
1. First-person point of view
Abilene (Tucker, probably)
2. First-person point of view
India Opal Buloni
3. Third-person point of view
4. Third-person point of view
5. Third-person point of view
6. First-person point of view
Black Beauty ("unknown from this excerpt, but inferred from the title")

Life Lessons (Page 53):
1. E   2. A   3. C   4. D   5. B

Which Genre? (Page 58):
1. non-fiction prose/biography
2. adventure novel/fantasy
3. mystery fiction
4. fantasy
5. horror fiction/science fiction
6. historical fiction
7. realistic fiction
8. folktale (tall tale)
9. science fiction

Solution to the Crossword Puzzle (Page 66):

Story Elements: Grades 3–6 Review (Pages 67–68):

1. suspense
2. exposition
3. climax
4. Flashback
5. Foreshadowing
6. Plot
7. Chronological
8. Conflict
9. cliffhanger
10. protagonist
11. dynamic
12. round
13. characterization
14. Setting
15. first-person
16. Mood
17. Tone
18. style
19. Theme
20. genres
21. static
22. symbol
23. flat
24. trait
25. resolution

Bibliography and Suggested Reading List

Babbitt, Natalie. *Tuck Everlasting*. New York: Farrar, Straus and Giroux, 1985.

Blume, Judy. *Tales of a Fourth Grade Nothing*. New York: Dell Publishing, 1972.

Carroll, Lewis. *Alice's Adventures in Wonderland*. New York: Barnes & Noble Classics, 2004.

Cleary, Beverly. *Dear Mr. Henshaw*. New York: HarperCollins, 1983.

Creech, Sharon. *Walk Two Moons*. New York: HarperCollins, 1996.

Curtis, Christopher Paul. *Bud, Not Buddy*. New York: Bantam, Doubleday, Dell, 2002.

Dahl, Roald. *Charlie and the Chocolate Factory*. New York: Penguin Books, 2002.

——. *James and the Giant Peach*. New York: Penguin Group, 2000.

De Angeli, Marguerite. *A Door in the Wall*. New York: Random House, 1998.

DiCamillo, Kate. *Because of Winn Dixie*. Cambridge, Massachusetts: Candlewick, 2000.

——. *Flora & Ulysses*. Cambridge, Massachusetts: Candlewick, 2013.

——. *The Tale of Despereaux*. Cambridge, Massachusetts: Candlewick, 2006.

Giff, Patricia Reilly. *Lily's Crossing*. New York: Random House, 1997.

Grahame, Kenneth. *The Wind in the Willows*. New York: Aladdin Books, 1989.

Hesse, Karen. *Out of the Dust*. New York: Scholastic Press, 1997.

Kinney, Jeff. *Diary of a Wimpy Kid*, The Long Haul. New York: Amulet Books, 2007.

Lowry, Lois. *Anastasia Krupnik*. New York: Dell Publishing, 1979.

——. *The Giver*. New York: Random House, 2002.

——. *Number the Stars*. New York: Random House, 1990.

Montgomery, L.M. *Anne of Greene Gables*. New York: Aladdin Books, 2001.

Naylor, Phyllis Reynolds. *Shiloh*. New York: Simon & Schuster, 2000.

Norton, Juster. *The Phantom Tollbooth*. New York, Random House, 2005.

O'Brien, Robert. *Mrs. Frisby and the Rats of NIMH*. New York: Aladdin, 1986.

O'Dell, Scott. *Island of the Blue Dolphins*. New York: Bantam, Doubleday, Dell, 1971.

Paterson, Katherine. *The Great Gilly Hopkins*. New York: HarperCollins, 1987.

Perrault, Charles. *Cinderella*. New York: Simon & Schuster, 1997.

Rawls, Wilson. *Where the Red Fern Grows*. New York: Bantam Books, 1997.

Riordan, Rick. *The Lightning Thief*. New York: Disney Hyperion, 2009.

Sachar, Louis. *Holes*. New York: Random House, 2001.

Sewell, Anne. *Black Beauty*. New York: Simon & Schuster, 2000.

Speare, Elizabeth George. *The Sign of the Beaver*. New York: Random House, 1984.

——. *The Witch of Blackbird Pond*. New York: Random House, 1978.

Spinelli, Jerry. *Maniac Magee*. New York: Little, Brown & Co., 1999.

Spyri, Johanna. *Heidi*. New York: Aladdin Classics, 2000.

Yates, Elizabeth. *Amos Fortune, Free Man*. New York: Penguin Books, 1989.

White, E. B. *Charlotte's Web*. New York: HarperCollins Publishers, 1952.

Made in United States
Orlando, FL
24 February 2024